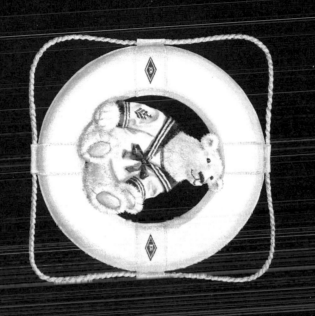

P9-CEV-883

"That's my tenth bear today," said the voice of a young woman proudly. Suddenly I felt myself being hurled through the air, then landing with a thump on a hard wooden bench. I opened my eyes and looked around the large, bright room littered with sawdust, tools and scraps of felt. On either side of a long table sat women who were quickly sewing black glass eyes onto teddy bears. I soon learned that they earned their living by making bears and other stuffed animals for toy shops around the world. Christmas was approaching, and they had been given a large order. This special lot of bears, including me, was to be shipped from Germany to America.

I wondered where America was and how I was to get there, but I didn't have long to wait.

There was a wonderful railway worked by electricity, and I could see a bright red engine going around and around, past flashing signal towers and stations.

An old advertisement for F.A.O. Schwarz.

A 1910 postcard of F.A.O. Schwarz's main store.

B ecause it was Christmastime, the shop was busy every day. My bear companions disappeared one by one, and I couldn't help wondering when my turn would come.

One day a lady with red cheeks looked me all over carefully, straightened my blue bow, and said she would take me along with her. I was sad to leave my lovely surroundings and hated being packed into a horrid little box again by one of the salesclerks.

For several days I was left in a closet. I thought everyone had forgotten me, but finally one morning the lady took me out of the box. Then we went down to the docks where we boarded a large ship called the *Caronia*.

The decks of the ship were crowded with people saying good-bye. As I looked about wondering what was to become of me, a little boy came running up.

Flinging his arms around the lady with the red cheeks, he cried, "Oh, Aunt Nannie, I wish you were coming with us!"

She gave him a big hug and then presented me to him. The little boy, my new master, had his father and mother with him and Nurse Burns, whom he called "Muddie Boons." Several people came down to see Master's family off, and I was admired by each one in turn, which made me feel very proud.

"How high he holds his head!" Master's father said. "What will you call him?"

"Polar," Master replied promptly.

Douglas's mother stands with some friends on the deck of the Caronia.

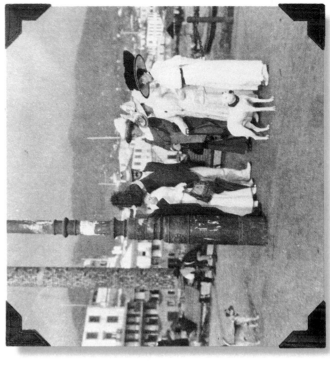

Reid's Palace Hotel was one of the finest places to stay in Madeira.

Tennis and walks around the harbor were part of a visit to the island.

A week later, we sighted the island of Madeira, near Portugal, which was to be our home for the next few months. It was a beautiful bright afternoon when we went ashore. We traveled through the busy streets to our hotel in a rickety old wooden cart pulled by a bull.

Our hotel was very grand. Master, Muddie Boons and I had a big sunny room overlooking the garden and the blue sea beyond.

I spent many lazy days out under the palms watching Master build little houses with sticks and stones and surround them with miniature gardens. And we rode in the bullock carts whenever we went up into the hills, exploring different parts of the island.

O ne sad day, Master woke up with red spots all over his face. "He's got measles," the doctor said gravely. "You'll have to put him in quarantine." Everyone looked very worried.

Master, Muddie Boons and I were moved to a little cottage a short distance from the hotel. Master's mother explained that being in "quarantine" meant staying away from the other guests so that we wouldn't give them measles.

We weren't in our new home for five minutes before a big brown mouse scampered across the floor. Poor Muddie Boons shrieked and went after it with a broom. She soon named our cottage "Mouse Castle" because it was full of mice, rats and ants, and she spent all her spare minutes trying to kill them. I didn't like my new quarters a bit, for Master was too sick to even notice me, and I was put in a corner and forgotten.

The doctor visited us often, and every day Master's parents came with fresh eggs and milk. Night after night, I watched as Muddie

"Mouse Castle,"
where Muddie Boons nursed Douglas.

Boons sat awake, holding Master's hot, limp hand in hers. A full week passed, and I began to wonder if he would ever be well enough to play with me again.

But one morning, I heard Master ask for me in a faint little voice. Muddie Boons handed me to him, and he put me on his pillow, and there I lay without stirring the whole day.

S lowly, Master began to grow stronger. He would sit up in bed, wash my face and paws, tie my ribbon and give me my breakfast. I was so happy to see him better that I almost didn't care what he did to me. But I didn't relish the bath Muddie Boons gave me one morning in a horrid, smelly liquid called disinfectant. She gave Master one, too. Then two men came to the garden with a hammock. They carefully lifted Master in as he held tight to his little American flag in one hand and me in the other. Muddie Boons led the way, and we all marched back to our own sunny room in the hotel.

Douglas is carried back to the hotel, where he rests on the balcony.

Soon Douglas is well enough to sit up and play. Here he is photographed with the doctor and with Maddie Boons.

21

Douglas and his family saw these huge locks being built for the Panama Canal. The postcard shows the great amounts of water that had to be controlled.

Douglas and his mother on the beach in Bermuda.

In the new year we sailed away to some hot, sunny places. We went to Panama, where a great canal was being built right through the country so that ships could sail from one side to the other. One of the engineers invited Master, Muddie Boons and me to ride out to see it in his big private car. Bright flocks of parrots flew from the trees as we roared down the jungle roads.

Bermuda was our last stop. Master took me to a beautiful beach where we

spent many a long afternoon. He would make a sort of throne out of sand for me to sit on and say, "Now, Polar, don't you run away, but just stay quiet while I work."

So I sat there
watching him
play and
sniffing the
salt air.

We took the night train to Paris. Strolling in the Tuileries Gardens, we saw boys sailing their boats in the fountains and watched hot-air balloons rising toward the sky. Master took me partway up the Eiffel Tower one day

and told me it was 984 feet high. He was always telling me the height and length of things.

I was sorry when it was time to go back to America, for I loved Paris. But Master was excited because we were to sail to New York on the *Titanic*, a magnificent new ship. Everyone said she was the biggest ship in the world. We were going to be on her very first voyage. The *Titanic* had left England

A postcard of the Titanic and one of the ship's diamond-shaped luggage stickers.

The Nomadic carried Douglas and his family out to the Titanic.

the day before and her first stop was at Cherbourg, France. We took a train to Cherbourg and that evening went out to the huge ship on a little tugboat.

As we stepped on board, the ship's doctor, who had known all of us on the Adriatic, kissed Master and said, "I see you still have Polar with you, little man!"

The lifeboat was swinging out from the ship's side, and people had difficulty climbing aboard. Our little party kept together, and when there were about forty of us in the boat, an officer cried, "Lower away," and we were let down to the water in awful jerks. Master clasped me in his arms. His eyes were shut tight, and his face was white. We finally reached the water safely and rowed off toward a faint light on the horizon.

It was very dark. Aside from the stars and the brilliantly lighted ship that towered above us, we could see nothing. Soon after we left the *Titanic*, the captain sent up rockets as a distress signal.

We all watched the ship steadily, except Master, who was asleep. Two hours later, we saw the last light go out and heard the dreadful cries that told us all was over. The great *Titanic* had gone down.

O ur rescue ship, the *Carpathia*, looked very small amidst the few bits of wreckage where the huge *Titanic* had gone down. We finally drew alongside, and the men climbed aboard the *Carpathia* on rope ladders. The women were hauled up in a sort of swing, and the children in canvas bags.

The Carpathia raced through the night to rescue the Titanic's passengers in the lifeboats.

Soon everyone had been rescued — except for me. I lay alone in the empty lifeboat. Several minutes went by, but nothing happened. Everyone seemed to have forgotten me. My heart began to pound. I imagined being left there, tossed by the waves forever. Would I ever see Master again?

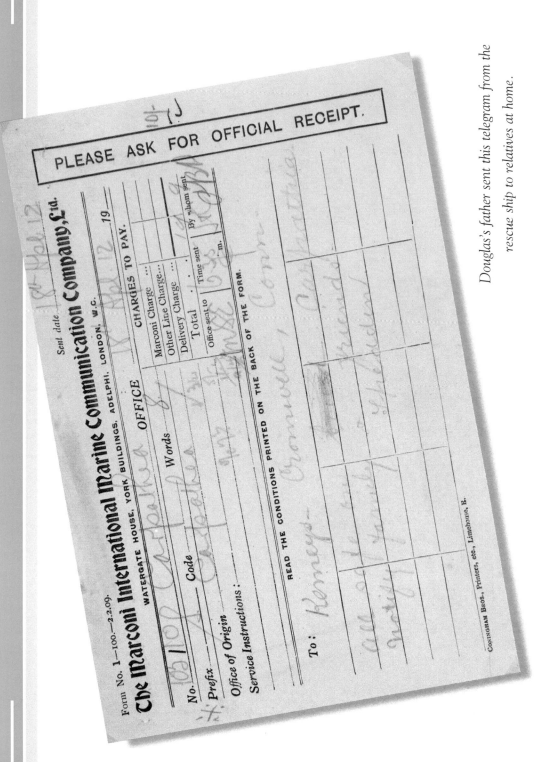

Douglas's father sent this telegram from the rescue ship to relatives at home.

"**P**olar!" a familiar voice shouted from across the room. It was Master. He rushed over and took me in his arms. I was delighted to see him again, too. But I was also rather upset to see that he was holding an ugly little brown bear. His mother had bought it for him in the ship's barbershop, thinking I had fallen overboard! As soon as Master saw me, however, he hugged and kissed me. He took me to bed with him that night and every night after, forgetting all about the other bear.

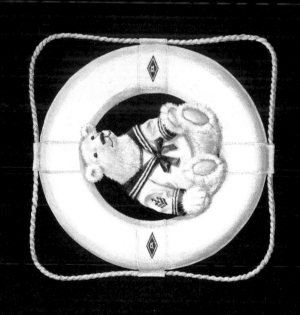